Prepper's Survival Pantry

The Ultimate How To Guide For Modern Day Emergency Food & Water Storage Including Safe Canning, Drying And Easy Recipes You Can Preserve.

By Urban Cheapskate Mom

Disclaimer:

The author and the publisher take no legal responsibility for any harm or loss, be it direct or indirect, resulting from using or implementing the information contained in this book as results may vary depending on the individual circumstances.
If you are unsure of any information contained in this book please consult a professional who specialises in the particular enquiry you have and can find the ideal solution relating to your particular situation.

Contents

Introduction

Chapter 1

How To Plan For The Short, Medium & Long Term

Chapter 2

How To Safely And Efficiently Store Water

Chapter 3

How To Safely And Efficiently Store Food

Chapter 4

Ways To Preserve Your Fresh Food Including Canning And Drying

Chapter 5

10 Delicious And Healthy Recipes You Can Easily Prepare And Preserve

Chapter 6

Ways To Properly Manage Your Food And Water In Case Of A Disaster Or Emergency

Chapter 7

Ways To Effectively Scavenge And Restock Your Supplies

Conclusion

Introduction

You have heard a lot about food storage lately and have begun to wonder if this is something you should get involved in. After all, your family is extremely important to you and you want to do all that you can to give them the best shot at a long and healthy life. That includes preparing to survive a

Supermarket shelves just prior to hurricane Sandy

disaster or other event that would have a negative impact on the food supply. Maybe your family suffers a financial setback or a family member gets sick and your budget is stretched thin.

No matter what the case is, having a supply of food on hand will go a long way to giving you peace of mind. You don't have to worry about putting food on the table when you are flat broke or worry about what you will feed the kids when the grocery store shelves are empty.

Building up an emergency food storage may seem like a hue feat that will take forever and cost you a small fortune. That doesn't have to be the case at all. This book will show you how to create a food storage without breaking the bank. You will learn about home preservation and how you can use it to save a ton of money by using the food you grow yourself.

It isn't just food you need to think about. Water is just as important, if not more so than food. A disaster, whether it be natural or man-made, will almost always disrupt the water supply. We rely on huge facilities to clean our water before it comes through our tap. Unfortunately, if the power is our or the water supply has been contaminated due to a major storm, your family won't have access to drinking water.

You need to store water for your family. Because it may not be possible to store enough water to last your family three months or more, you need to also consider ways in which you will clean any water you collect from outside sources.

You may be thinking, "this is a lot to do and think about!" and it is, but this book will take you by the hand and help you develop an emergency food storage plan that will sustain your family.

Despite all the prepping, you may find you run short on supplies if the disaster stretches on. This book will give you some tips to help you stretch your food supply as well as ways to supplement your food storage. Learn what to eat first and what to save for last and how you can keep your family fed with very little.

There is a lot to do, but taking it one step at a time will get the job done.

Chapter 1

How To Plan For The Short, Medium & Long Term

Planning for Emergencies

Emergencies and disasters are, by their very nature, unexpected. It is impossible for us to know ahead of time when a severe storm will down power lines and cut out electricity for millions of people, or when an earthquake or tornado will strike. The unpredictability of such events does not mean that you can't make preparations to make certain that your family will have adequate food and water to make it through a disaster.

This chapter will discuss some of the things you will want to consider when planning for short, medium, and long-term emergency situations. For example, in the short-term things like expiration dates and nutritional value are not as necessary as they would be for a longer emergency. Whatever the situation, ensuring you have adequate supplies to get by without outside assistance will be your top priority.

Short-Term Planning

A short-term emergency is a situation that endures from a few hours to two weeks. The food and water you have stored for this type of emergency should be easily accessible. During a short term power outage or disaster, if you have access to your refrigerator you will want to eat refrigerated foods first. Bacteria grow very quickly once the temperature of the refrigerator goes over 40 degrees Fahrenheit, so it is imperative to have a supply of shelf-stable food and clean drinkable water. Water is especially important. Bear in mind that each member of your family needs a gallon of drinking water every day. In some disasters, water supplies may not be a problem. However, it's a good idea to have enough bottled water on hand to keep your family going for two weeks. Make sure to include extra for rehydrating and cooking food.

When you are choosing foods to store for emergencies, select items that are ready-to-eat. If you have camp stove or grill that you will be able to use, then you can plan on being able to heat some things. However, unless you are positive that you will be able to cook food all the way through, stick to things that you can eat as they are. Commercially canned foods are a good choice, since they do not require cooking or refrigeration. You might also consider things like jerky, dried fruit, nuts, granola bars, and shelf-stable milk and juice.

During short-term emergencies, you may want to give some thought to nutrition but it's more important to focus on calories and comfort foods. Comfort foods are foods that are high in carbohydrates, which your body will need during an emergency situation. Make sure to plan for your family members' particular needs when you are considering what supplies to get. Don't forget medications, first-aid supplies, and foods that will meet any special dietary concerns. If you have a small baby who drinks formula, make sure to include prepared formula. If you decide to put away powdered formula, remember that you will need extra water in order to use it. Make sure to set aside food for your pets as well. Finally, make sure to include a can opener and scissors so you can open the food that you have stored.

Medium-Term Planning

Medium-length disasters are those which last anywhere from three weeks to three months. Hurricane Katrina is an example of this kind of emergency. Flooding from the storm closed roads, making it difficult for public safety workers to get through, and people were without water for an extended period. Depending on where you live, you may want to plan for this kind of emergency. It may be helpful to buy a few extra items each week, so you can work your expenditures into your budget. You already know that each person in your family will need a gallon of drinking water per day. Most of us do not have sufficient storage space to set aside enough water for an extended period. If you are concerned about being without drinkable water, it's a good idea to include some water purification tablets with your emergency supplies. These are iodine tablets that will turn contaminated water into potable water in a short period. Make sure to review the label of any tablet you buy and calculate how many pills you will need for your family.

For medium-term emergencies, you will want to think about the nutritional needs of your family. Stock a variety of foods. While you will want to include the same things you would for a short-term emergency (canned and dried foods) you may also want to think about including cereals, dried beans, and powdered milk. You can also consider preserving food for use during these situations, something we'll talk about in detail later in this book. You will also want to think about variety here as your family won't want to eat the same canned goods every day for months.

Long Term Planning

A long-term emergency is one that lasts longer than three months. If you think you need to prepare for this kind of emergency, you will need to take a lot of things into consideration. You may want to buy some water barrels to store water. You might also want to consider including clothing, blankets, over the counter medicines, and other things to ensure your family's comfort. If you are stockpiling large amounts of food, it's important to date everything and go through your stored food regularly. Make sure to use items that are about to expire first, and then replace them with fresh items.

Your needs may vary, but here are some guidelines to consult if you are planning to store enough food to last your family for a year. You may decide not to worry about sugar, for example, and to store extra canned goods or other items instead. These guidelines are intended to serve as a starting place for you.

Table of how much foods needed per person during an emergency

Item	Over 7	Child <7	Notes
Grains	300 lbs	128 lbs	Includes wheat, rice, oats, flour, pasta, cereals
Legumes	75 lbs	24 lbs	Includes all kinds of beans, as well as peanuts
Meat	150 lbs	70 lbs	Includes canned and dried meats
Milk	75 lbs	37 lbs	Includes evaporated and dry milk
Sugars	60 lbs	29 lbs	Includes sugar, honey, molasses, and agave
Fruits	185 lbs	92.5 lbs	Includes fresh, canned, and dried fruits
Vegetabl-es	185 lbs	92.5 lbs	Includes fresh, canned, and dried vegetables
Fats & Oils	25 lbs	13 lbs	Includes shortening, vegetable oils, and nut oils
Salt	5 lbs	3 lbs	Includes iodized salt, kosher salt, and sea salt
Baking powder	1 lb	1 lb	
Baking soda	1 lb	1 lb	
Yeast	.5 lb	.5 lb	
Vinegar	.5 gallons	.5 gallons	

Other Considerations

While food and water are necessary, they are not the only issues to think about when preparing for an emergency. If you are planning to store a large amount of food, you will need to be diligent in terms of keeping track of expiration dates. Maintain a complete list of the food you have stored and review it periodically. It may help to keep older food toward the front of your storage area and use it as the expiration dates approach.

For long-term preparedness, it's a good idea to include a variety of over-the-counter medications, personal hygiene products, and first-aid items. Here are some suggestions of products you may want to store.

Medications

- Pain relievers such as aspirin or ibuprofen

- Cough and cold medicine

- Cough drops

- Antacid tablets

- Allergy pills

First Aid Items

- Band-aids and gauze bandages

- Antibiotic ointment

- Rubbing alcohol

- Hydrogen peroxide

- Cortisone cream

- Antifungal ointment

Personal Hygiene Products

- Shampoo and Conditioner

- Toothpaste

- Extra toothbrushes

- Dental floss

- Petroleum jelly

- Safety razors

- Hand sanitizer

It may be helpful to do a little basic meal planning for the long term and group foods for meals together for easy access. You can even note down cooking instructions, and other ingredients needed – such as water. Make sure to include disposable plates and utensils, because if you are reliant upon your stored water you won't want to use it to wash dishes. Don't forget cooking vessels and utensils. The more specific you are in your preparation, the less likely it is that you'll wind up being unprepared.

Chapter 2

How To Safely And Efficiently Store Water

Conserving Your Water Supply

After an emergency, you may be without running water, or water supplies may become contaminated. This chapter will talk about how to safely store water, and how to purify water in the event that you run out of potable water.

Prepare an Emergency Water Supply

The primary thing to remember is the basic guideline of one gallon of drinking water for each person, per day. You will need to make sure to include sufficient water for your pets as well, and you can use the same guideline.

You will need to switch your drinking water supplies every 6-12 months. Observe the expiration of store-bought water to make sure it is safe to consume. Treat stored water the same way you would food – keep track of when you stored it, and rotate it out as necessary. Try to replace stored water every six months. It is best to have water not already opened, which is the most secure and reliable source of water during a disaster.

You can buy containers in surplus stores and store the water yourself. Be sure to find containers that are airtight. Avoid jugs that can break such as glass bottles. Label drinking water jugs with "Drinking Water" and additional water with "For Other Water Purposes." Keep the water stored in a cool, dry place – in particular, avoid storing

containers in an area that gets direct sunlight.
Plan water supplies for instant oatmeal, instant pudding,
dried soups, dry milk, powdered drink mixes, bouillon
cubes or powder, instant rice, and instant potatoes.

Keeping Your Water Safe

How can you make sure that the water you've stored is safe
for human consumption? Contaminated water is a
significant problem during emergencies, especially when
flooding has occurred. In this section, we will discuss what
steps you can take to keep your water clean and free of
contaminants. Make sure to filter cloudy water before
purifying it – you can do this by pouring it through a coffee
filter or clean rag.

The best way to purify
contaminated water is to boil
it. Boiling kills disease-
causing organisms such as
viruses and bacteria. If you
have a stove and pots in
which to boil the water, this is
the best choice. However,
during an extended
emergency, boiling water may
not be possible or practical.
Fortunately, there are other
ways to make contaminated water safe.

You can use regular household bleach with a chlorine
content between 5.25% and 8.25%. Make sure to check the
label and only use bleach that has no added perfumes or

dyes. Use the following guidelines to determine the quantity of bleach you will need.

- 1 quart/1 liter   5 drops bleach

- 2 quarts/2 liters/half gallon   10 drops bleach

- 1 gallon   ¼ teaspoon

- 5 gallons   1 teaspoon

- 10 gallons   2 teaspoons

After adding the bleach, stir the water well. Wait for a minimum of an hour before you drink it. You can also add two drops of bleach per gallon to stored water to keep it fresh for a longer period.

Make sure to store purified water in a thoroughly clean airtight container to avoid contamination. Here are some easy steps you can take to clean and sanitize your water containers before filling them.

- Using dishwashing soap and water, wash the water storage container, and make sure you rinse it completely with clean water.

- Make a solution by mixing a teaspoon of unscented liquid household chlorine bleach in a quart of water. Pour the mixture into your container and cover it. Shake it well, making sure that the solution touches all inside surfaces of the container.

- After 30 seconds, pour the solution out of the container

- Air dry the empty sanitized container before use or rinse the container again with clean water.

- Avoid containers that can break such as glass bottles. It's better to use unbreakable containers made of plastic or metal.

- Make sure to use containers that you can seal tightly. Storing water in a container that allows air or liquid seepage may result in contaminated water. It's important to keep your water supply safe from contaminants.

- Never use a container that previously contained liquid or solid chemicals, including bleach.

- Cardboard or plastic bottles, jugs, and containers used for fruit juices or milk are not ideal for water storage.

Choosing the right container and preparing it in a proper way is the key to a safe emergency water supply.

Chapter 3

How To Safely And Efficiently Store Food

Safeguarding Your Food Supply

Now that you know how to ensure a safe supply of potable water for your family, it's time to get into more detail with your food storage. You know that you will need to stockpile shelf-stable foods, but supplies of this kind still need to be stored properly.

Choosing Food Storage Containers

- Always make sure to use a food grade container when storing your emergency food – this is to make sure that non–food chemicals that are harmful to human health will not transfer. Food grade containers do not contain any chemicals that are hazardous to human health. If you are uncertain about a particular container, you can attempt to contact the manufacturer for additional information. If you cannot verify if the container is safe, do not use it.

- For foods like pasta, noodles, cereals, and other dried foods, you can use different sizes of plastic storage containers. Use containers made of polycarbonate and polyethylene which are especially for dehydrated and dried foods.

- For storing bulk, dry emergency foods like wheat, rice, beans, oatmeal, flour, and sugar, food storage buckets work great.

Additional Protection for Sealed Containers

For long-term food storage, you may want to take some extra precautions to ensure the freshness and safety of your food. These measures will keep your food safe from contaminants. Plastic containers or buckets will keep oxygen out for a longer period than glass or metal will, but nothing will keep pests out forever. You've probably experienced the irritation of having pests get into staple foods like flour or sugar. There are a few things you can do to minimize the chances of this happening.

- You can use oxygen absorber packets and or desiccant packets. But you need to remember that these packets are not edible, they are only intended to keep your dry goods dry and edible. You can buy these packets online at Amazon.com and uline.com

- You can use oxygen barrier bags inside your plastic containers. Metalized oxygen barrier bags (Mylar) are best for light and insect control. Make sure to get food-grade bags. Uline.com is an excellent source for storage containers.

- Food Grade Diatomaceous Earth is an organic, edible pest control substance made from fossilized diatoms. It is widely available online and in gardening supply stores. If you are storing grain or beans, mix one copy of diatomaceous earth into 25 pounds of beans or grain.

Foods to Consider Storing

The first chapter discussed possible food choices in a general way. Here are some more concrete suggestions of things you might want to think about including with your emergency provisions.

Canned Food Items

- Meals such as stew, chowder, chili, ravioli, spaghetti, and chow mein

- Fruits: choose fruits packed in water or natural juices, not in thick syrup

- Protein: water-packed tuna and chicken

- Vegetables: beans, peas, corn, carrots, tomatoes (whole, purees and sauce), etc.

Dehydrated items

- Pasta such as spaghetti, macaroni & cheese, lasagna

- Soups or soup mixes

- Dried fruits

- Dried meats (jerky)

Staples

- Flour, sugar, cocoa, cornmeal, powdered milk

- Salt, pepper, seasonings and spices

- Rice, uncooked cereals

- Breakfast cereals

- Vinegar

- Baking soda

- Cooking oil

- Crackers

- Instant beverages like tea, hot chocolate, cider and coffee.

- Condiments

- Special diet foods for the elderly, infants (baby food), diabetics and those with allergies.

- High energy foods: peanut butter, granola, nuts

- Comfort foods: candies, cookies, hard candies and nuts.

Chapter 4

Ways To Preserve Your Fresh Food Including Canning And Drying

You can use several different methods to preserve fresh foods inexpensively by canning, drying, or freezing them. Once you understand the basic procedures, you can use them to make sure you have nutritious food available for your family in emergencies.

Canning

The first preservation method to consider is canning. Canning involves putting food into sanitized jars and vacuum sealing it to keep out contaminants and bacteria. While commercially canned foods can be a useful staple, they also tend to contain preservatives, chemicals, and large amounts of salt. If you preserve foods yourself, you can guarantee that the food you are storing is free of chemicals and unhealthy ingredients. There are two similar techniques you can use to can your food.

Water-bath canning

Water bath canning or hot water canning, is a process of canning that uses boiling water in a large kettle. Simply put, it involves placing filled jars into the water and boiling them until the jars have reached an internal temperature of 212° Fahrenheit for

a specific duration of time. Water bath canning is an excellent method to use for fruit juices, jellies, jams, fruits, fruit spreads, salsa, tomatoes with added acid, sauces, pickles and condiments. Here is a step-by-step guide to water bath canning:

1. Read through your recipe and instructions, and prepare the ingredients and equipment. Follow the guideline for the jar size, recipe preparation, and the processing time.

2. Quality check – Check jars, lids, and bands to ensure they are safe to use. Jars with irregular rims, cracks, nicks, or sharp edges may prevent sealing or be liable to break. The underside of the lids should not be uneven or have incomplete sealing compound as this may result in improperly sealed jars. Make sure that the band fits your jar perfectly.

3. Clean jars, lids, and bands in hot soapy water, rinse well, and dry.

4. Place the jars in hot (not boiling) water until you are ready to use them. Fill a large saucepan or a stockpot half-way with water. Ensure that the jars are fully submerged, leaving them full of hot water. You may also use dishwashers to clean and heat jars. Keep the jars hot when adding the hot food; this will prevent the jars from breaking. Leave the bands and lids in a room temperature for easy handling.

5. Prepare tested preserving recipes using fresh produce and other quality ingredients

6. Remove the jars from the hot water using a jar lifter; make sure to empty the water inside. Fill each jar

with prepared food, and don't forget to leave headspace.

7. Remove any air bubbles in the food. You can use either a bubble remover and a headspace tool or a rubber spatula. Slide it between the jar and the food to release the trapped air. Repeat 2 – 3 times.

8. Wipe the outside of the jars with a damp cloth to remove any food residue. You can now proceed with applying the bands, making sure to seal them tightly.

9. Place the filled jars in the canner until canner is full. Lower rack with jars into the water, making sure to submerge each jar entirely in the water. Put the lid on the canner, and bring the water to a full rolling boil.

10. Process the jars in the boiling water for the time indicated on your recipe. When the process is complete, you can now turn the heat off and remove the canner lid. Let the jars stand in the canner for around 5 – 6 minutes to get it acclimated to the outside temperature.

11. Remove the jars from the canner and set them upright on a towel to prevent the jar from breaking due to the sudden change in temperature. Leave the jars undisturbed for 24 hours.

12. Lastly, check the seals on the lids. The lids should not flex up or down when you press the center. Once you have tested them, you can remove the bands, and try lifting off the lids with your fingertips. If the seal is good, you will not be able to lift the lid. Note that if

the lid does not seal properly, you can still refrigerate or reprocess the product.

13. Clean the lids and mason jars.

14. Label your preserves. Make sure to include the date so you can use food before it expires. Store it in a cool, dark, and dry spot for up to a year.

Pressure canning

To use this method of canning, you will need a large kettle that produces steam in a locked compartment. You will need to heat your filled jars to an internal temperature of 240° internally under a particular pressure measured by a dial on the canner cover. Pressure canning is an ideal method for processing vegetables and low acid foods such as meat, poultry and fish. Here are step-by-step instructions for pressure canning.

1. Ready the pressure canner as needed, including jars, lids, ring bands, and other helpful accessories.

1. Wash jars, lids and bands in hot soapy water, rinse well and dry.

2. Heat the jar in hot water until it's ready for use. Follow instructions listed above under water bath canning.

3. Fill the clean hot jars one at a time. You can consider reheating the jars if necessary, simply by immersing the jar in the canning kettle that is full of hot water.

4. Remember to leave at least an inch of headspace to allow for expansion of the food.

5. Take out any air bubbles that have formed. You can use either a bubble remover and a headspace tool or a rubber spatula. Use the same method you would use for water bath canning.

6. By using a clean damp cloth, carefully wipe the jar rim. Any food residue around the rim may prevent the jar from sealing properly.

7. Remove lids from the hot water and carefully place them on the jars. Plunge the lids into cold water, if the lids stick together; then dip them again in boiling water. Screw the ring bands on as tightly as you comfortably can.

8. Place a rack in the canner and fill it halfway with hot (not boiling) water.

9. Place jars on a rack so the steam can flow around them freely. Do not pack the jars too tightly.

10. Securely fasten the canner lid.

11. Heat the canner to the highest setting until the steam flows from the vent port or petcock.

12. Keep the heat on high for at least ten minutes as steam flows, and then close the petcock. It will

pressurize for the next 3 to 5 minutes.

13. Start timing the process and watch the dial gauge until it shows that the interior has reached the recommended pressure.

14. The weighted gauges should rock about two to three times per minute. For presto canners, they should rock slowly during the entire process.

15. Turn the heat off. Remove the canner from heat to let the canner depressurize.

16. Never force-cool canners. Force-cooling will result in food spoilage or loss of liquid from the jars.

17. Once the canner has depressurized, open the petcock. Wait for about 2 minutes, unfasten the lid, and carefully remove it. Make sure to keep the lid away from your face to avoid getting burned.

18. Remove the jars from the canner and set them upright on a towel to prevent the jars from breaking. Leave the jars undisturbed for 24 hours.

19. Lastly, check the lids to make sure they are tightly sealed and do not flex up or down when you press the center. Once you have checked the seals, you can remove the bands, and then test the lids to make sure you cannot easily remove them. Remember, even if the lid has not sealed properly, you can refrigerate or reprocess the product.

20.   Put on a label, making sure to include the date. Store your preserved food in a cool, dark, and dry

place for up to a year.

Drying

Drying food is the one of the oldest methods of preserving food. People have been drying food for centuries, and it is a simple, inexpensive way of keeping food edible for a long time. As with canning there are several different methods you can use.

Sun Drying

The oldest and most inexpensive way to dry food is by using the heat from the sun. This method works best for fruits, because they have a high amount of acid and sugar. This method is not optimal for drying meats and vegetables.

Ideal conditions for sun drying your food include a temperature of about 85° F. Drying foods on a day with a constant light breeze is preferable since the flow of air will help lift moisture from the fruit. Very humid weather is not a good time to attempt drying food as humid air has a high moisture content that may lengthen the drying time. Humidity of 60% or less lends itself to this form of drying. If you live in place where it tends to be very humid, you may want to stick to using a dehydrator or your oven. If you decide to try sun drying food, use this method:

1. Prepare the equipment needed in the sun drying process. You'll need a rack or screen. Placing food on a rack will ensure adequate airflow around the

food. Placing the racks or screens on top of concrete surfaces or aluminum sheets will help by increasing the temperature. The higher the temperature is, the more rapidly the food will dry.

2. Make sure to use food-grade quality materials for the racks or screens. Screens made of Teflon–coated fiberglass, stainless steel or plastic are ideal for sun drying. Avoid racks or screens made of copper, hardware cloth or aluminum, which are hazardous to human health.

3. Protect the drying fruits from insects and birds. You can use another screen or cheesecloth to keep pests away from your food.

4. Leave the fruit under the sun until it is completely dry. Because heat, weather and humidity can slow the process down, you will have to keep an eye on the fruit. Once it is entirely dry, store the fruit in an airtight container.

Food Dehydrators

For foods with a low acid content such as meats and vegetables, a food dehydrator is your best option for preserving foods. The convenient thing about using a dehydrator is that it takes away much of the guess-work. You can just follow the  manufacturer's instructions for drying food. As with sun-dried foods, store the dried meats and vegetables in airtight containers and make sure to date them so you can rotate out food before it goes bad.

Conventional Oven

If you don't own a food dehydrator, you can also dehydrate foods in your oven, as long as it can hold a consistent temperature under 200 degrees. The ideal temperature is 140 degrees. Slice, trim and blanch the food first. Then put it in a single layer onto a baking sheet. Place it into the oven with the door open several inches to allow moisture to escape. Drying times vary for different foods, so make sure to do your research.

With any dried foods, make sure to watch it for several days after you have dried it. If you notice any moisture accumulating on the inside of the storage container, the food is not completely dry. It may require a little bit of experimentation to do this properly, but it's an excellent method to ensure your family will have adequate food.

Chapter 5

10 Delicious And Healthy Recipes You Can Easily Prepare And Preserve

Canned Recipes

Canned Black Bean

First you need to soak the required amount of the bean in water at least 8 hours before making it.

- 1 cup black bean
- 2-3 medium Onions
- 3-4 medium size tomatoes
- 4 garlic cloves
- 1 1/2 Tbsps. Salt
- 4 Tbsps. Oil
- 1/2 Tbsp. cumin seeds
- Small piece of ginger

First we are going to keep the black beans for boiling in a deep pan on a medium flame so that it gets tender. Put cup of water into one 1 cup of black beans, and then add ½ Tbsp. of salt so that the bean should dissolve the salt until the black beans get tender and soft, we will make the gravy.

For the gravy, first, we have to grind the onions, ginger, and garlic cloves to make an excellent paste. Then pour oil into the pan and add cumin seeds in the hot oil; after the cumin seeds get roasted add the grind paste in the oil. Now roast the paste till it gets little brown, in the meantime grind the tomato and add them in the paste. Now roast the paste till it leaves the oil after that add boiled black beans with enough water to make it thicker. Now it can be stored in a freezer and can use for future.

Canned Spinach

- 1 bundle of spinach
- Salt to taste
- 4 onions
- Piece of ginger
- 2-3 green chilies
- 4-5 garlic cloves
- Whipped cream

Wash and cut the spinach. Now add 1 cup of water in a pan and add spinach to it, cover it and keep it on medium flame. Then make a paste of onions, ginger, green chilies, and garlic cloves. After that heating oil in a pan, add the paste and make it till brown. Grind the spinach (if it gets tender and soft). Now add the spinach in the paste and keep it in a slow flame for about 10 minutes. When the spinach and water get mixed together, store it in a can for the future.

Gravy Cauliflower

- 1 Cauliflower
- 2-3 onions
- 3 tomatoes

- 3-4 Cashew nuts

- Salt to taste

- Oil for fry

- 3-4 black pepper

- ½ Tbsp. cumin seeds

- 2 bay leaves

- 2-3 cloves

- 1 cardamom seeds

First, we will cook the cauliflower in a pan (do not deep fry). After that, put the cauliflower aside on butter paper, so that the oil gets absorbed. Next, warm the oil in a pan, put in cashew nuts, cumin seeds, bay leaves, black pepper, cloves, and cardamom seeds. Now, roast them, cut the onions, and mix it in the pan, until the onions get brown, and then add tomatoes and mix it well. When the tomatoes get tender, add a cup of water, and bring it to boil. Later add the fried cauliflower and mix it well. You can store it in a can for further use.

Canned eggs

- 2 Eggs

- 3 onions

- 3 tomatoes

- Salt to taste

- 4 black pepper

- ½ Tbsp. cumin seeds

- 1 bay leaf

- 3 cloves

Boil the eggs in a pot with enough water to cover them. Grind the onions and tomatoes. Next, heat oil in a pan and add black pepper, cumin seeds, bay leaf, cloves. Now sauté them. Then add grind paste in the pan once the paste gets brown add 2 cups of water and let it boil for 5-8 minutes until the paste and water get mixed well. Peel off the egg shells and cut them into two pieces and add them into the pan. After one more boil cut turn the stove off and let it sit until it cools down, then store it in a can for future use.

Gravy Cheese

- 2 Potatoes

- Cheese

- Coriander leaves

- Piece of ginger

- 3 Onions

- 3 garlic cloves

- ½ Tbsp. cumin seeds (roasted)

- Oil for fry

- Salt to taste

- Pinch of turmeric

First, boil the potatoes. Then, peel the potatoes and mash them like a paste, now add salt coriander leaves, roasted cumin seeds and grated cheese. Just make small balls of the mixture and heat the oil in a pan for frying them. Do not deep fry the balls; just let them cook a little brown. Now, pour the oil in another container and leave 2 Tbsp. oil in a pan, add chopped onions, garlic cloves, grated ginger, and a pinch of turmeric to make them brown, add a cup of water, and then boil it for 5 minutes. After 5 minutes, add 2 cup of water and let it boil for five more minutes. Then, you add the light brown balls to the pan and put on the lid. Once it cools down store it in a can for future.

Dried Recipes

Lady Finger

- Lady Fingers ½ lbs.
- 2 Tbsp. Olive oil
- 2 Tbsp. Spoon tomato puree
- ¼ Tbsp. cumin seeds
- Powdered black pepper ¼ tsp spoon
- Salt to taste
- ½ tsp turmeric powder
- Coriander leaves

Wash the Lady Fingers, wipe with a clean cloth, cut the top, and a bit from the bottom, then cut into ½ inch pieces. Cut the onion into thin pieces and take the Non-stick pan and place it on the stove. Pour the olive oil and heat it, low the flame, add cumin seeds and roast till light brown. Now add chopped onion, and lady fingers add turmeric and black pepper powder mix well. Put the lid on the pan and let the vegetable cook for 3 minutes. Then pour the tomato puree, and then cook on medium flame for 2 minutes. Cook on low flame for the last 3 minutes once you mix the mixture for 2 minutes. Next, you can cut the stove off when it is done. Garnish with coriander leaves.

Vegetable Pasta

- Bowl of Pasta
- Onion   medium sized 3 cut into 4 pieces each
- Carrot ½ cups, cut into thin one inches pieces
- Cabbage chopped ½ cup
- French Beans ½ cup cut into ½ inches small pieces
- Garlic 6 cloves paste
- 1 Tbsp. powdered black pepper
- Tomato puree
- Salt to taste
- Olive oil 1 Tbsp.
- Mustard seeds 1 Tbsp
- Chili flakes ½ TspWater (as a requirement)
- White vinegar 2 Tbsp. Spoon

Take the Non-stick pan, pour enough water to dip pasta, add a pinch of salt, ¼ Tsp of olive oil, place the pan on high flame and boil for 2 minutes. Then remove the pan from the stove and sieve the water, pour cold water (so pasta won't stick). Once again place the pan on a high flame, add remaining oil, heat it, add mustard seeds till light brown, and then put onion season for a minute mix garlic paste.

Later, put all the vegetables in and mix well for 3 minutes, and then mix the pasta, pour the puree, salt, black pepper and vinegar, mix lightly well for 2 minutes. Garnish with chili flakes.

Mix Vegetables

- Chopped cabbage ¼
- Very small pieces of carrot ¼
- Capsicum cut into round shaped ¼
- Peas pods ¼
- Evenly cut small pieces of French beans ¼
- Pieces of boiled cauliflowers
- 4 mushrooms
- Grated Cheese ½ cup
- Salt to taste

Pour the oil into the pan, heat it, then pour the oil on the vegetables and turn the flame on high mix the vegetables in the oil and roast them for five minutes. Now add salt, cheese and seasoning of your choice. Garnish with coriander leaves

Dry Potatoes

- 3 potatoes
- ½ Cumin seeds
- Coriander leaves

Pour the washed potatoes in a deep pan with enough water

to cook. Make sure you cook them on high flame for 10 minutes, but when the water begins to boil lower the flame to medium for 15 minutes. After 15 minutes check the potatoes to ensure they are done. Then take them out of the water and peel them. Heat oil in a pan, add cumin seeds until they crack, cut the potatoes in fine pieces, and add it in a pan with salt. Next, mix it well and close the flame and garnish with coriander leaves.

Chapter 6

Ways To Properly Manage Your Food And Water In Case Of A Disaster Or Emergency

Now that you know how you can store a sufficient stockpile of water and food for your family, it's time to talk about how to make those supplies last in the event of a disaster.

Water

As previously mentioned, it is critical not to ration water unless you need to. Going without water is much more dangerous than going without food. Make sure each person in your family, and each pet, has enough water to drink.

While you want to make sure to drink enough water in a day, you also want to make sure not to waste it. If you have bottled drinking water, use that only for drinking and cooking. You do not need to use potable water for bathing or doing laundry. If you do not have running water, you might consider washing dishes in clothes in a stream if there is one nearby.

If you are concerned about running low on water, there are some simple things you can do to help conserve it. Never ration water, but if you reduce your physical activity and keep your body cool, you may find that you need to consume less. If the weather is hot, try to stay indoors or in the shade.

Food

Depending on where you live, replacing your food supplies may be more difficult than replacing the water. In order to make your food last as long as possible, you will want to be strategic about what you eat, and when you eat it. If the power goes out, make sure to eat refrigerated foods first. There is a short time frame when you will be able to eat those foods – usually only four hours or so. Save your non-perishable items for later when you will need them. Next, eat frozen foods. If you can cook, you can cook them. If you cannot cook, just defrost what can be eaten without cooking and eat that. Only when you have exhausted your supply of refrigerated and frozen food should you turn to the non-perishable and shelf-stable items you have stored. Note that if it is cold outside, you may be able to prolong the lifespan of refrigerated or frozen foods by removing them from the refrigerator bringing them outside. If there is snow on the ground, take advantage of it and bury your food in it, or gather snow and pack it into a cooler and put your food in too.

Another way to make food last is to work out daily menus in advance. If you have an idea of how many calories each family member needs, you'll have a better idea of how much food to store. Sometimes we eat more than we need if we are scared, tired, or bored. You can help prevent overeating by doing other things to keep yourself occupied. You might consider playing a game with your family, or coming up with interesting conversation topics.

The right knowledge on how to manage your food during an emergency is the key to survival.

Chapter 7

Ways To Effectively Scavenge And Restock Your Supplies

If you are in a short-term emergency situation, you will probably not have to worry about running out of supplies. However, if an emergency situation stretches on for weeks or months, even the best-prepared family might find their emergency supplies running low. Let's talk about some ways to restock your supplies and scavenge for more.

Water

If you find your water supplies running low, here are some simple suggestions for where you can find more, both inside and outside your home. You will want to shut off the main water valve in your house to keep the water from becoming contaminated.

Inside the house

- Melted ice cubes (make sure they are from clean water, or treat the water before drinking.)

- Water from inside your water heater.

- Water from inside the toilet tank (not the bowl.)

- Liquids from canned fruits or vegetables.

Outside the house

- Rainwater – collect in a clean container

- Water from natural sources, including rivers, streams, ponds, lakes, and natural springs

Make sure to boil or otherwise treat any water you receive from outside your home. If you are unsure about water inside the house, treat that too. It is better to unnecessarily treat safe water than to skip this step and consume water that is not safe.

Food

If your food supplies start to run low, you may need to look for more. Chances are the obvious places – supermarkets and bulk goods stores – will be empty because people who need food will go there first. It's a good idea to know all of the businesses in your area where you might be able to find food. Think beyond supermarkets and include gas stations and convenience stores, restaurants, malls, and department stores.

You might want to consider keeping a guide to local wild edibles with your supplies in case you need to forage for food. If you do this, make sure to think about the tools you will need to help you find food. Including a shovel or rake, gloves and other implements may help you. It may be worthwhile to take the time to learn what wild edibles are in your area now, before disaster strikes. A lot of essential plants are edible. Some things to look for are greens, like dandelion greens, fruits, nuts, berries, and tubers. Identification is imperative, so if you are unsure about the safety of a particular food, don't eat it.

Another option to consider is hunting. If you are already a hunter, simply include hunting supplies such as guns, ammunition, snares, and fishing tackle with your emergency supplies. If you are not a hunter, you can still learn how to build a simple snare that will help you catch wildlife. You may even be able to catch fish with a net.

It's important to note that some of these options for foraging can also help you extend the life of your non-perishable food as you go. If you hunt and gather as you go, you'll be able to make better use of your stockpiled food and it will last longer.

Conclusion

Nobody likes to sit around and think about disaster scenarios and horrifying what-if situations, but it isn't wise to completely ignore the possibilities of a natural disaster, act of war or economic collapse. Anything can happen. While we hope for the best, we must prepare for the worst.

If nothing ever happens, it isn't like the food will go to waste. It can be used as a supplement to your regular pantry as long as you replace what you use. Think of it as the stocked shelves in your local supermarket. Because you need to keep your food supply fresh, you will want to pull out stuff that is getting old and use it in your kitchen and replace the old stuff with new stock.

The skills you learn, like dehydrating and canning food, are invaluable. There is no doubt food prices will continue to rise. You can save your family a ton of money by making home preservation a habit. You will be able to take pride in the fact you are feeding your family food you have packaged with love and without a lot of nasty chemicals and other potentially harmful preservatives.
You will also be handing down skills to your children who will see the benefits of having an emergency food storage and make it a practice in their own homes with their own families. These are lessons you want to pass down to your children. Lessons that will help them live that long life we all envision for our children.

Today is the day you start planning for your future. You don't have to do it all at once, but you do need to take that first step. Come up with a strategy and start making plans to begin your emergency food storage the next time you go to the market. Little by little your storage will be built up and you will feel better for it. Get your family involved and your job will be that much easier.

From The Author

Thank you for taking the time to read this book. As an author, I understand the importance of creating books which my readers will find both enjoyable and informative. If you have the time and feel generous, please don't hesitate to leave an honest review of this book..........Urban Cheapskate Mom

Other Books By Urban Cheapskate Mom

Low Carb On A Budget

Eating healthy low carb meals is easy and budget friendly if you follow the recipes and tips inside this book.

No need to buy expensive meal plans or spend hours trudging through lists of do's and don'ts when this handy guide full of recipes has done the work for you. Discover foods you may not have considered before and learn ways to keep your diet in check. Healthy eating is a choice that shouldn't wreak havoc on your bottom line.

How To Dry Herbs At Home

Have you ever wondered if it was hard to dry herbs in your own kitchen?

Maybe you remember your grandmother hanging herbs around her kitchen and you remember the lovely aroma she always had in the house, even when she wasn't making dinner. Drying herbs is such an easy task, it is something we should all be doing. You will get a sense of satisfaction when you harvest your home grown herbs from your garden and dry them for long term food storage. When you need some spice for your recipe, it is exciting to reach into the cupboard and use the seasoning you prepared in your own kitchen. Your meals will be more enhanced and you will never go back to those boring store-bought spices again.

Drying herbs is easy, but there are some key details you need to know. There are so many different methods you can use to dry the herbs, you need to know which is best for you and the herbs you grow. This book will explain the various techniques along with the different types of herbs and how they should be dried. Not all herbs are created equal and not all herbs should be dried the same. This book will help you determine the best way to go about it.

You will also learn about shelf lives and storing methods. Each step of the drying process determines how long and how powerful your herbs will be. Don't take chances by winging it. This book will take you step by step through the harvesting to the storing of your herbs. You will be a professional by the time you are done reading this book, which means you have an excellent shot at turning your dried herbs into a lovely extra income! We could all use that!

www.ingramcontent.com/pod-product-compliance
Lightning Source LLC
Chambersburg PA
CBHW070504290526
45790CB00003B/1088